MEDITERRANEAN
COOKING

TORMONT

Graphic Design: Zapp

This edition published in 1996 by:
Tormont Publications Inc.
338 Saint Antoine St. East
Montreal, Canada H2Y 1A3
Tel. (514) 954-1441
Fax (514) 954-5086

ISBN 2-7641-0107-4
Printed in Canada

CONTENTS

APPETIZERS
AND SOUPS

It would be easy to devote an entire book to the appetizers and soups of the Mediterranean. In fact, in some countries, including Greece, Turkey and Lebanon, appetizers are of the utmost importance and easily compose a meal in themselves.

As for soups, they range from the delicately flavored Avgolemono to some of the more robust fish soups for which the Mediterranean is justifiably famous. Be sure to look at the Fish and Seafood section as well, as our variation of the famous Bouillabaisse is so hearty that it's really a main course!

Baked Vegetable Salad, Crostini (page 6)

Baked Vegetable Salad

1	eggplant, halved and sliced	1
2	red bell peppers, cut in thick strips	2
1	green bell pepper, cut in thick strips	1
1	onion, sliced	1
1/2 cup	olive oil	125 mL
	fresh basil for garnish	

◆ ◆ ◆

1 Preheat oven to 350°F (180°C). Place the eggplant slices, pepper strips and onion slices in a well-greased baking dish. Drizzle oil over, then bake in the oven for 20 minutes, basting regularly.

2 Arrange vegetables on a serving dish and garnish with fresh basil.

Serves 4

TIP: *This simple dish derives its rich flavor from olive oil, so buy the best oil you can afford. Extra virgin olive oil will produce a much fresher flavor than regular olive oil, which is extracted with heat.*

Crostini

1	loaf French bread	1
2	tomatoes, seeded and finely chopped	2
1 tsp	olive oil	5 mL
2	anchovy fillets, finely chopped	2
2 tbsp	capers, drained	30 mL
1 tbsp	finely chopped fresh basil	15 mL
6 oz	mozzarella cheese, thinly sliced	180 g

◆ ◆ ◆

1 Slice the bread into 1/4 inch (5 mm) thick slices. Combine tomatoes, oil, anchovies, capers and basil.

2 Cover bread slices with a slice of mozzarella and top with a spoonful of the tomato mixture.

3 Grill crostini under a preheated broiler until cheese has just melted. Serve hot.

Serves 4-6

TIP: *Crostini is one of those infinitely variable recipes that is easy to adapt with your own personal touch. Try using different types of cheese and herbs.*

Spinach and Feta Filo Triangles

| 12 | sheets filo pastry, 18 × 12 inch (45 × 30 cm) each | 12 |
| 6 tbsp | butter, melted | 90 mL |

FILLING

1	onion, chopped	1
2 tbsp	olive oil	30 mL
8 oz	frozen spinach, thawed	240 g
4 oz	feta cheese	120 g
6 oz	cream cheese	180 g
2	eggs, beaten	2
3 tbsp	fresh breadcrumbs	45 mL

♦ ◆ ♦

1 Preheat oven to 375°F (190°C). In a skillet, fry onion in oil over medium heat until soft. Add spinach, mix well and cook until liquid has evaporated, stirring occasionally.

2 Crumble feta into a bowl. Add cream cheese and eggs; mix well. Stir in breadcrumbs and spinach mixture.

3 Stack filo sheets and cut them with scissors into 12 × 2 inch (30 × 5 cm) strips. Work with one strip at a time (covering the remaining strips with a tea towel).

4 Brush the filo strip generously with melted butter. Place a heaping teaspoonful of filling at one end of strip, so that the corner of the strip can be folded over it diagonally to make a triangle. Continue folding strip over on itself, maintaining the triangular shape. Brush with melted butter and place on a baking sheet.

5 Repeat, using remaining filo and filling. Bake triangles for 10-12 minutes or until golden. Serve hot or warm.

Makes about 60 triangles

Lamb and Spinach Mustard Strudel

3 tbsp	olive oil	45 mL
1	large onion, finely chopped	1
3/4 lb	lean lamb, finely diced or ground	350 g
2 cups	finely chopped mushrooms	500 mL
2 tbsp	Dijon mustard	30 mL
1 cup	frozen chopped spinach, thawed, drained and squeezed dry	250 mL
1	red bell pepper, finely chopped	1
2 tbsp	chopped fresh parsley	30 mL
3/4 cup	fresh breadcrumbs	185 mL
6	sheets filo pastry	6
1 tbsp	sesame seeds	15 mL
	salt and freshly ground pepper	

1 Preheat oven to 350°F (180°C). Heat 2 tbsp (30 mL) oil in a skillet over high heat. Add onion and lamb and brown on all sides.

2 Stir in mushrooms and cook for 2 minutes. Transfer mixture to a large bowl. Add mustard, spinach, red pepper, parsley and breadcrumbs to lamb mixture. Season to taste and mix thoroughly.

3 Brush each filo sheet with oil before stacking them together. Spoon lamb mixture along the short side of the filo stack, about 1 inch (2.5 cm) from the edge. Roll up filling in the filo to a firm sausage shape. Tuck edges under and place seam side down on a baking sheet.

4 Brush with remaining oil. Sprinkle with sesame seeds. Bake 40 minutes or until golden. Slice to serve.

Serves 6-8

TIP: Filo can be bought frozen in the freezer department of most large supermarkets. Tightly rewrap and refreeze unused portions at once.

Italian Mussel Soup

4 tbsp	olive oil	60 mL
1	garlic clove, finely chopped	1
2 cups	chopped canned tomatoes	500 mL
2 1/2 cups	puréed tomatoes	625 mL
1/4 cup	dry white wine	60 mL
1 tbsp	chopped fresh basil	15 mL
24	mussels, scrubbed and bearded	24
1/4 cup	light cream	60 mL
	freshly ground pepper	

◆ ◆ ◆

1 Heat the oil in a large saucepan over low heat. Add garlic and cook for 2 minutes. Stir in chopped tomatoes, puréed tomatoes, wine and basil. Simmer 15 minutes.

2 Add mussels, discarding any whose shells are open. Cover pan, raise heat to high and steam mussels about 5 minutes or until shells open.

3 Transfer mussels to a bowl, remove them from their shells, then return them to the soup, along with any mussel juices. Stir in the cream and pepper to taste, and serve with more chopped fresh basil if desired.

Serves 4

TIP: Buy good-quality canned tomatoes, preferably plum tomatoes, for this recipe. Canned tomatoes are usually fairly salty, so you will probably not need to add any salt to this soup.

Avgolemono Soup

6 cups	chicken stock	1.5 L
6 tbsp	long-grain rice	90 mL
4	egg yolks	4
1/4 cup	fresh lemon juice	60 mL
1 tbsp	chopped fresh parsley	15 mL
	salt and freshly ground pepper	

◆ ◆ ◆

1 Bring chicken stock to a boil in a large saucepan. Add rice and cook for 15 minutes or until rice is tender.

2 In a bowl, beat egg yolks with a rotary or electric beater until pale and creamy. Add lemon juice and mix well.

3 Strain the rice, reserving the stock. Set aside 3/4 cup (185 mL) stock in a measuring cup. Pour remaining stock into a clean saucepan and simmer until needed. Reserve the rice.

4 Slowly pour 1/4 cup (60 mL) of the measured stock into the egg and lemon mixture, stirring well. Stir in the remaining 1/2 cup (125 mL) stock, then slowly pour the egg mixture into the saucepan of simmering stock, stirring constantly until the soup thickens.

5 Add reserved rice to the soup, season with salt and pepper to taste, garnish with parsley and serve.

Serves 6

Sweet Pepper Salad

3	red bell peppers	3
4 tbsp	olive oil	60 mL
1 tbsp	red wine vinegar	15 mL
1 tbsp	fresh lemon juice	15 mL
1 tbsp	liquid honey	15 mL
1 tbsp	yellow mustard seeds	15 mL

◆ ◆ ◆

1 Place peppers under a preheated broiler, and broil, turning occasionally, until all skin is charred. Place peppers in a paper bag until cool, then rub off charred skin and cut out seeds and membranes. Slice peppers into strips and arrange in a shallow dish.

2 Whisk olive oil, vinegar, lemon juice, and honey together in a small bowl. Stir in mustard seeds and pour over peppers.

3 Cover dish and chill the salad for at least 3 hours before serving to allow flavors to blend.

Serves 4

TIP: *Red peppers treated this way will store, covered, up to 1 week refrigerated. They make a great addition to an antipasto platter or to cold meat sandwiches.*

Carpaccio *with Mustard Mayonnaise*

1 lb	best quality beef fillet, all fat removed, sliced wafer-thin	450 g
	lettuce leaves	
	watercress	

MUSTARD MAYONNAISE

1	egg	1
1 tbsp	fresh lemon juice	15 mL
2	garlic cloves, finely chopped	2
2 tsp	Dijon mustard	10 mL
1/4 cup	olive oil	60 mL

♦ ◆ ♦

1 Arrange sliced fillet and lettuce leaves decoratively on four individual plates. Arrange watercress on top.

2 To make the mustard mayonnaise, process egg, lemon juice, garlic and mustard in a blender or food processor until well mixed. With the motor running, add oil in a thin stream through the feeder tube until the mayonnaise thickens.

3 Spoon some of the mustard mayonnaise over each serving of carpaccio. Serve immediately.

Serves 4

TIP: *Since the beef is eaten raw, it is essential that it be scrupulously fresh and from a reputable butcher. Place the fillet in the freezer for about 1 hour, until partially frozen, to make slicing it easier, and use a razor-sharp knife.*

Antipasto Platter

8	radicchio leaves	8
8	spinach leaves	8
8	slices bread, cut into rounds	8
8	slices salami	8
8	slices mozzarella cheese	8
1	cucumber, with skin	1
1	roasted red pepper (see page 10)	1
1/2 cup	black olives	125 mL
1/4 cup	sun-dried tomatoes in oil, drained	60 mL
1 tbsp	chopped fresh basil	15 mL
1/2 cup	stuffed green olives	125 mL
8	canned baby corn cobs	8
1/2 cup	olive oil	125 mL
5 tbsp	white wine vinegar	75 mL

♦ ♦ ♦

1 Arrange radicchio and spinach leaves on a large platter. Toast bread rounds. Place a slice of salami then a slice of mozzarella on each round and grill until cheese melts. Arrange on platter.

2 Using a potato peeler, cut cucumber, into long lengthwise strips. Twist each strip, then arrange on platter as shown.

3 Slice roasted pepper into strips, and place in a bowl. Add black olives, sun-dried tomatoes, and basil. Mix well. Arrange on platter. Add green olives and corn to platter.

4 Make a dressing by whisking together oil and vinegar. Drizzle over vegetables on platter, avoiding cheese and salami toasts.

Serves 4

Dolmades

6 oz	vine leaves, drained	180 g
2 tbsp	butter	30 mL
1	onion, chopped	1
1	garlic clove, finely chopped	1
1/2 cup	long-grain rice, cooked	125 mL
2 tsp	grated lemon zest	10 mL
1/3 cup	slivered almonds, toasted	85 mL
1	egg, lightly beaten	1
	salt	

◆ ◆ ◆

1 Rinse vine leaves under cold water and drain thoroughly.

2 Heat butter in a saucepan over medium heat. Add onion and garlic and cook until tender, stirring occasionally. Remove from heat. Stir in rice, lemon zest, almonds, egg and salt to taste.

3 Place 2 tsp (10 mL) of mixture on each vine leaf. Roll up firmly, tucking in edges. Place rolls close together in a saucepan. Add water to cover. Simmer, covered, for 30 minutes. Drain and chill before serving.

Makes about 24

TIP: Prepared vine leaves can be purchased in packages or jars in specialty shops and large supermarkets. You can also use fresh vine leaves — pick young pale-green leaves and blanch them in boiling water 4 to 5 minutes until color darkens, then drain.

Taramasalata

2 ¹/₂	slices white bread, crusts removed	2 ¹/₂
¹/₂ cup	milk	125 mL
2	garlic cloves, finely chopped	2
¹/₄ cup	fresh lemon juice	60 mL
4 oz	smoked cod roe, skinned	120 g
¹/₄ cup	olive oil	60 mL

◆ ◆ ◆

1 Put bread in a shallow bowl, add milk and set aside to soak for 5 minutes.

2 Transfer bread and milk to a food processor. Add garlic, lemon juice and cod roe. Process until smooth.

3 With motor running, add oil, at first drop by drop, and then in a steady stream. Spoon mixture into a bowl, cover and chill at least 30 minutes before serving. Serve with French bread or pita and garnish with fresh dill if desired.

Serves 4

Tzatziki

1	large cucumber	1
2 cups	Greek yogurt or plain low-fat yogurt	500 mL
1 tbsp	finely chopped fresh mint	15 mL
1 tbsp	finely chopped fresh parsley	15 mL
2	garlic cloves, finely chopped	2

♦ ♦ ♦

1 Peel cucumber and grate coarsely. Stir in remaining ingredients. Cover and refrigerate at least 1 hour. Serve with pita or French bread for dipping.

Serves 4

Hummus

1 cup	dried chickpeas	250 mL
1/2 cup	tahini (sesame paste)	125 mL
1/2 tsp	salt	2 mL
1/4 tsp	freshly ground pepper	1 mL
1/4 cup	fresh lemon juice	60 mL
3	garlic cloves, finely chopped	3
1/3 cup	ricotta cheese	85 mL
3 tbsp	olive oil	45 mL
	paprika	
	chopped fresh parsley	

♦ ♦ ♦

1 Cover chickpeas with water and let soak 4 hours. Drain chickpeas and place in a large saucepan. Cover with fresh water and bring to a boil. Simmer 1-1 1/4 hours or until tender. Drain, reserving 1 cup (250 mL) cooking water.

2 In a food processor, purée chickpeas with the reserved cooking water, tahini, salt, pepper, lemon juice, garlic and ricotta until smooth.

3 Spoon hummus onto a shallow plate, sprinkle with paprika and parsley and drizzle with olive oil. Serve with pita bread.

Serves 6

TIP: To save time, use 2 cans of chickpeas instead of dried chickpeas. Drain them, and use 1 cup (250 mL) water instead of the cooking liquid.

Harlequin Tomatoes

2 tbsp	mayonnaise	30 mL
12	large tomato slices, 1/2 inch (1 cm) thick	12
12	slices mozzarella cheese, cut in rounds	12
6	slices cucumber, halved	6
6	pitted black olives, halved	6
	flat-leaf parsley	

PESTO

1/2 cup	chopped fresh basil	125 mL
1	garlic clove, chopped	1
1/4 cup	pine nuts	60 mL
2 tbsp	olive oil	30 mL
2 tbsp	grated Parmesan cheese	30 mL

♦ ♦ ♦

1 To make the pesto, place all ingredients in a blender or food processor and blend until well mixed. Stir in mayonnaise.

2 Arrange tomato slices on a platter or individual plates. Top with pesto mayonnaise. Add a mozzarella slice and a half cucumber slice to each. Garnish with half an olive and a sprig of parsley.

Serves 4-6

FISH AND
SEAFOOD

Lands bounded by the Mediterranean share a common bounty: the sea's rich harvest. From simple steamed shellfish to richly flavored stews, famous dishes like paella and bouillabaisse have made a valuable contribution to international cuisine.

Many of the wonderful recipes in this chapter combine fish or seafood with the diverse vegetables and herbs of the Mediterranean region, including tomatoes, saffron, oregano and mint.

The people of the Mediterranean are thrifty users of the sea's harvest; follow their lead and select the best fresh fish and seafood you can find, rather than always sticking to the ingredients called for in the recipes.

SPANISH SEAFOOD CASSEROLE (PAGE 20)

Spanish Seafood Casserole

1	frozen uncooked lobster tail, thawed	1
2 tbsp	olive oil	30 mL
2	onions, chopped	2
1	small green bell pepper, chopped	1
1	small red bell pepper, chopped	1
2	garlic cloves, finely chopped	2
2	tomatoes, chopped	2
1 cup	water	250 mL
1/2 cup	dry white wine	125 mL
5 tbsp	brandy	75 mL
2 tbsp	fresh lemon juice	30 mL
2	bay leaves	2
1 lb	raw shrimp, unpeeled	450 g
1 lb	mussels or clams, scrubbed and bearded	450 g
2 tbsp	chopped fresh parsley	30 mL
	salt and freshly ground pepper	
	pinch saffron	

◆ ◆ ◆

1 Cut lobster meat into large chunks. Heat oil in a large saucepan over medium-high heat. Stir-fry onions, peppers and garlic for 2 minutes.

2 Add tomatoes and cook 5 minutes. Stir in water, wine, brandy, lemon juice, saffron and bay leaves. Bring to a boil, then lower heat and simmer 1 minute.

3 Add lobster, shrimp and mussels. Cook over low heat until mussels have opened and shellfish is tender. Discard any shellfish that remain closed. Season to taste and serve at once, garnished with parsley.

Serves 4

Shrimp with Feta

1	small onion, finely chopped	1
1 tbsp	butter	15 mL
1 tbsp	olive oil	15 mL
1/2 cup	dry white wine	125 mL
4	tomatoes, peeled, seeded and chopped	4
1	garlic clove, chopped	1
1 tsp	chopped fresh oregano	5 mL
4 oz	feta cheese, crumbled	120 g
2 lbs	raw shrimp, peeled and deveined	1 kg
4 tbsp	chopped fresh parsley	60 mL
	salt and freshly ground pepper	

◆ ◆ ◆

1 In a large saucepan, cook onion in butter and oil over medium heat for 5 minutes. Add wine, tomatoes, garlic and oregano. Season with salt and pepper.

2 Bring to a boil, then lower heat and simmer until sauce thickens slightly. Add feta cheese, stir well, then simmer 10 minutes, stirring occasionally.

3 Add shrimp and cook over medium heat until shrimp turn pink. Do not overcook. Transfer to a serving dish and sprinkle with parsley. Serve immediately.

Serves 4

Quick Paella

1/4 cup	olive oil	60 mL
2	garlic cloves, finely chopped	2
1	onion, chopped	1
3	tomatoes, chopped	3
1	red bell pepper, chopped	1
1 lb	cooked chicken, cut in bite-size pieces	450 g
1 tsp	paprika	5 mL
1/4 tsp	powdered saffron	1 mL
1 1/2 cups	long-grain rice	375 mL
3 cups	chicken stock	750 mL
1 cup	peas, thawed if frozen	250 mL
1/2 lb	peeled cooked shrimp	225 g
	salt and freshly ground pepper	

1 Heat oil in a large deep skillet. Add garlic, onion, tomatoes and red pepper. Cook over medium heat, stirring frequently, for 5 minutes. Add chicken, paprika and saffron.

2 Level mixture in pan, spread rice evenly on top and cook for 3 minutes. Pour stock into mixture and stir.

3 Bring to a boil and cook for 10 minutes. Season to taste with salt and pepper. Add peas and shrimp and continue cooking until most of the liquid has been absorbed and rice is tender. Serve hot.

Serves 4

Bourride

4 tbsp	butter	60 mL
2	onions, sliced	2
2	large parsnips, sliced	2
4 cups	chicken or fish stock	1 L
1 cup	dry white wine	250 mL
1/4 cup	freshly squeezed lime juice	60 mL
1 tsp	crushed black peppercorns	5 mL
3/4 lb	sea bream (dorade) or seabass filet, cut in large chunks	350 g
3/4 lb	mussels, scrubbed and bearded	350 g
1/4 cup	sour cream	60 mL
1 1/2 tbsp	chopped fresh dill	25 mL
	salt	

◆ ◆ ◆

1 Heat butter in a large saucepan over medium heat. Add onion and parsnips and cook for 2 minutes, stirring constantly.

2 Add stock, wine, lime juice, pepper, fish and mussels. Bring the mixture to just below boiling point (bubbles should barely break the surface). Cover, lower heat and simmer until the mussels open. Discard any mussels that remain shut.

3 Using a slotted spoon, remove the mussels, fish and vegetables. Shell the mussels. Add sour cream to broth remaining in pan. Season to taste with salt. Simmer until mixture is reduced by half and begins to thicken.

4 Return mussels, fish and vegetables to pan. Stir in dill and heat gently. Serve at once.

Serves 4

Calamari with Tomato Mint Sauce

3 tbsp	olive oil	45 mL
2 tbsp	finely chopped garlic	30 mL
1/2 tsp	crushed black peppercorns	2 mL
1/4 tsp	hot chili paste	1 mL
3/4 cup	drained canned chopped tomatoes, puréed	185 mL
1/4 cup	dry white wine	60 mL
1 tbsp	tomato paste	15 mL
3/4 lb	small calamari (squid) rings	350 g
1 tbsp	chopped fresh mint	15 mL

◆ ◆ ◆

1 Heat oil in a large saucepan. Add garlic, pepper, chili paste, puréed tomatoes, and wine and cook for 3 minutes over medium-high heat.

2 Stir in tomato paste and calamari and cook, stirring, for 2 minutes. Stir in mint and serve.

Serves 4

TIP: *Squid should never be overcooked, as it tends to toughen.*

Spinach Noodles *with* Scallops Provençale

1 1/2 lbs	fresh sea scallops	675 g
1/4 cup	milk	60 mL
1 1/2 lbs	tomatoes, peeled and coarsely chopped	675 g
2	bay leaves	2
1 cup	water	250 mL
1/2 tsp	dried thyme	2 mL
1	small onion, sliced	1
1 lb	spinach fettucine	450 g
2 tbsp	butter	30 mL
1 tbsp	finely chopped garlic	15 mL
2 tbsp	chopped fresh parsley	30 mL
	salt and freshly ground pepper	

♦ ♦ ♦

1 Place scallops in a bowl, add milk and set aside. Place tomatoes in a saucepan over medium heat and heat through. Add 1 bay leaf with salt and pepper to taste. Cook 5 minutes. Remove pan from heat and set aside.

2 Drain scallops. Discard milk. Place 1 cup (250 mL) water, remaining bay leaf, thyme and onion in a large skillet and bring to a simmer. Add scallops and poach them gently for 2-3 minutes or until scallops are opaque. Remove scallops from liquid using a slotted spoon, drain well and add them to tomato mixture.

3 Cook pasta according to package directions and drain. Melt butter in a small saucepan over low heat. Add garlic and cook, stirring constantly, until it begins to brown.

4 To serve, place noodles in a large serving dish, top with scallop tomato mixture, drizzle with garlic butter and sprinkle with parsley.

Serves 4

Shellfish Bouillabaisse

¹/₄ cup	olive oil	60 mL
2	onions, chopped	2
1	large celery stalk, sliced	1
2	garlic cloves, finely chopped	2
1	carrot, sliced	1
1	bay leaf	1
³/₄ cup	dry white wine	185 mL
4 cups	chopped canned tomatoes with liquid	1 L
1 cup	chicken stock	250 mL
¹/₂ cup	tomato paste	125 mL
¹/₂ lb	calamari (squid) rings	225 g
1 lb	clams	450 g
¹/₂ lb	cooked peeled shrimp	225 g
1	cooked lobster, meat coarsely chopped, tail shell reserved	1
2 tbsp	chopped fresh parsley	30 mL

♦ ◆ ♦

1 Heat oil in a large saucepan over medium heat. Add onions, celery, garlic, carrot and bay leaf. Cook, stirring constantly, for 5 minutes. Add wine and cook until reduced by half. Stir in tomatoes, stock and tomato paste. Simmer 15 minutes.

2 Stir in calamari and clams. Simmer 5 minutes or until clams have opened. Discard any that remain closed.

3 Add cooked shrimp and lobster meat and heat through for 1 minute. Remove bay leaf. Sprinkle soup with chopped parsley and garnish with the lobster tail. Serve at once.

Serves 4

TIP: Serve with rouille: whisk together 2 egg yolks, 2 crushed garlic cloves, 1 tsp (5 mL) sugar and a little salt and pepper, then slowly whisk in 1 cup (250 mL) olive oil, drop by drop, until mixture is thick and creamy.

Scallops with Parsley and Wine Sauce

1 lb	sea scallops	450 g
2	garlic cloves, finely chopped	2
1 tbsp	chopped fresh oregano	15 mL
6 tbsp	olive oil	90 mL
1 1/4 cups	dry white wine	310 mL
6 tbsp	dry breadcrumbs	90 mL

◆ ◆ ◆

1 Combine scallops, garlic, oregano and 4 tbsp (60 mL) olive oil in a large bowl. Cover and refrigerate for 1 hour.

2 Heat remaining olive oil in a medium skillet. Add scallops with marinade and cook over high heat 2 minutes.

3 Add wine and breadcrumbs and stir vigorously 1 minute.

4 Serve at once, garnished with lemon slices and chopped fresh parsley.

Serves 4

Seafood Salad

3/4 cup	dry white wine	185 mL
1/4 cup	fresh lemon juice	60 mL
2 tsp	finely chopped hot chili pepper	10 mL
1/2 lb	sea scallops	225 g
1/2 lb	calamari (squid) rings	225 g
1 cup	water	250 mL
1 lb	mussels, scrubbed and bearded	450 g
1 lb	cooked peeled large shrimp, tails intact	450 g
1/4 cup	olive oil	60 mL
3 tbsp	fresh lime juice	45 mL
1 tbsp	chopped fresh basil	15 mL

◆ ◆ ◆

1 Combine wine and lemon juice in a large saucepan. Bring to a boil, add chopped chili pepper, scallops and squid and cook 2 minutes. Using a slotted spoon, transfer scallops and squid to a bowl. Set aside.

2 Add 1 cup (250 mL) water to liquid remaining in pan. Bring to a boil. Add mussels and steam until shells have opened. Discard any that remain shut. Using a slotted spoon, remove mussels and set aside to cool.

3 Shell mussels. Add mussel meat to scallops and squid. Bring liquid in saucepan to a boil, then simmer until reduced to about 1/2 cup (125 mL). Let cool.

4 Stir shrimp into seafood mixture in bowl. Add olive oil, lime juice and basil to saucepan and mix well. Pour mixture over seafood in bowl. Toss lightly, then cover and let marinate in refrigerator 4 hours before serving.

Serves 6

Pickled Octopus Salad

12	baby octopus, tentacles only, cleaned and cut into lengths	12
1 1/2 cups	white wine vinegar	375 mL
1/4 cup	sugar	60 mL
3	small cucumbers, sliced	3
1	red bell pepper, cubed	1
1 tsp	yellow mustard seeds	5 mL
2 tbsp	chopped fresh dill	30 mL

◆ ◆ ◆

1 Combine octopus, vinegar and sugar in a medium saucepan over medium heat. Bring to a boil, add cucumber and red pepper and cook for 2 minutes. Using a slotted spoon, transfer octopus, cucumber, and red pepper to a bowl. Let cool.

2 Bring vinegar mixture to a boil, lower heat and simmer for 5 minutes. Cool to room temperature. Add to octopus and vegetables. Stir in mustard seeds and dill. Cover and chill until ready to serve.

3 Arrange octopus and vegetables on serving plates. Pour a little of the vinegar marinade on top and serve.

Serves 6

Crab Sauté *with* Prosciutto

2 tbsp	butter	30 mL
1/2 lb	cooked crabmeat	225 g
2	green onions, finely chopped	2
1 tbsp	chopped fresh parsley	15 mL
1/4 tsp	freshly ground black pepper	1 mL
1 tbsp	fresh lemon juice	15 mL
1/4 tsp	chili paste or 1 tsp (5 mL) chopped chili pepper	1 mL
8	slices prosciutto	8

♦ ♦ ♦

1 Melt butter in a medium saucepan over medium heat. Stir in crab, green onions, parsley, pepper, lemon juice and chili paste. Cook for 1 minute.

2 Arrange 2 slices of prosciutto on each of 4 plates, then divide the crab mixture between them. Garnish with lemon and parsley and serve at once.

Serves 4

TIP: *The number of live crabs to buy depends on their type and size; for example, a 5 oz (150 g) hard-shell crab will produce about 1 1/2 oz (45 g) of meat. If you are lucky, your fish dealer carries cooked crabmeat, which will save you a lot of bother.*

Meat
and Poultry

In many Mediterranean countries, meat is regarded as a luxury item, to be treated with respect. Because it is more expensive than in North America, it is often accompanied with vegetables and flavorful sauces — a practice which has the bonus of being healthier too!

In Italy, tender cuts such as veal cutlets are sealed quickly in hot oil, then cooked until perfectly tender before being served with a sauce made from the pan juices. (If you're not fond of veal, you can cook boneless chicken breasts or thin pork cutlets the same way.)

The French excel at slow-cooked dishes featuring beef or poultry, while in Greece, lamb is the favored meat.

Beef with Sun-Dried Tomatoes, Veal Picatta (page 32)

Beef *with* Sun-Dried Tomatoes

6 oz	jar sun-dried tomatoes in oil	180 g
1 lb	thinly sliced round steak	450 g
2 tbsp	olive oil	30 mL
1	red onion, chopped	1
2	garlic cloves, chopped	2
1	tomato, finely chopped	1
1/2 lb	pattypan (custard) squash, quartered, or zucchini, sliced	225 g
2 tsp	finely chopped fresh rosemary	10 mL
2 tbsp	tomato paste	30 mL
1 1/2 cups	chicken stock	375 mL
1/4 cup	dry white wine	60 mL
1 tsp	cornstarch	5 mL
1 tbsp	chopped fresh parsley	15 mL
	salt and freshly ground pepper	

♦ ♦ ♦

1 Drain the sun-dried tomatoes, reserving 4 tbsp (60 mL) of oil. Cut the steak into thin strips.

2 Heat the oil from the tomatoes in a medium skillet. Add beef and cook over high heat 2-3 minutes. Remove beef with a slotted spoon and set aside.

3 Add olive oil to skillet. When hot, add onion, garlic, tomato, squash or zucchini, rosemary and tomato paste. Cook for 2 minutes over medium heat.

4 Stir together stock, white wine and cornstarch until cornstarch is dissolved. Add to skillet and cook, stirring, about 10 minutes, or until reduced by half.

5 Stir in beef strips, sun-dried tomatoes and parsley. Season to taste. Heat through for 1-2 minutes before serving.

Serves 4

Veal Picatta

1/4 cup	all-purpose flour	60 mL
8	medium veal cutlets, tenderized	8
4 tbsp	butter	60 mL
1/2 cup	fresh lemon juice	125 mL
1/2 cup	dry white wine	125 mL
1	lemon	1

♦ ♦ ♦

1 Lightly flour the veal cutlets on both sides. Shake off excess.

2 Melt butter in a large skillet over medium heat. When the butter bubbles, add the veal and fry for 2 minutes on each side. When the veal is almost cooked, sprinkle on the lemon juice. Using tongs, transfer veal to a serving dish and keep hot.

3 Add wine to skillet and boil over high heat, stirring constantly until liquid is reduced to about 1/2 cup (125 mL). Pour sauce over veal.

4 Cut lemon into paper thin slices and place 3 slices on each cutlet. Serve immediately.

Serves 4

TIP: *Veal cutlets can be tenderized by pounding them with a wooden mallet or the flat side of a cleaver to break down the tougher fibers.*

Osso Buco

1 tbsp	olive oil	15 mL
4	veal knuckles or shank slices, 3/4 inch (2 cm) thick	4
2	onions, chopped	2
2	carrots, diced	2
2	celery stalks, diced	2
2	garlic cloves, chopped	2
2 tbsp	chopped fresh parsley	30 mL
1/2 cup	dry white wine	125 mL
2 cups	chopped canned tomatoes	500 mL
1/4 cup	tomato paste	60 mL
1 cup	chicken or veal stock	250 mL
	salt and freshly ground pepper	

GREMOLATA

1	garlic clove, finely chopped	1
2 tbsp	chopped fresh parsley	30 mL
1 tsp	grated lemon zest	5 mL

♦ ♦ ♦

1 Heat oil in a large, heavy-based pan. Add veal and brown on all sides over medium-high heat. Remove veal and set aside.

2 Add onions, carrots, celery, garlic and parsley and cook, stirring, for 5 minutes.

3 Add wine, and stir, scraping bottom of pan. Stir in tomatoes, tomato paste and stock. Season to taste. Bring to a boil.

4 Return veal to pan, cover and simmer 1 1/2-2 hours or until veal is very tender. Transfer to a serving dish.

5 Stir together the gremolata ingredients. Sprinkle over veal before serving.

Serves 4

Venetian Liver with Herbs

3 tbsp	butter	45 mL
3	garlic cloves, finely chopped	3
2	large red onions, cut in wedges	2
6 tbsp	all-purpose flour	90 mL
1/2 tsp	crushed black peppercorns	2 mL
1/2 tsp	salt	2 mL
2 tbsp	finely chopped fresh herbs	30 mL
1 1/2 lbs	calf's liver, cut in thin strips	675 g
1	red bell pepper, cut in thin strips	1
	fresh basil for garnish	

♦ ♦ ♦

1 Melt 1 tbsp (15 mL) butter over medium-high heat in a large nonstick skillet. Add garlic and onions. Cook 2 minutes. Transfer to a plate and set aside.

2 Combine flour, peppercorns, salt and half the chopped herbs in a bowl. Add liver and toss to coat.

3 Melt remaining butter in skillet. Add red pepper and cook for 1 minute over medium-high heat. Remove and add to onion.

4 Add liver to pan, increase heat to high, and cook, stirring occasionally, until liver is cooked as desired. Return onion and red pepper mixture to pan along with remaining chopped herbs. Heat through, and serve garnished with fresh basil.

Serves 4-6

TIP: *Be careful not to overcook calf's liver, as it will toughen. At its best, the inside is still slightly pink.*

Pork with Artichokes

2 tbsp	olive oil	30 mL
1	onion, chopped	1
1	garlic clove, finely chopped	1
1/4 tsp	coarsely ground black pepper	1 mL
1 1/2 lbs	pork fillet, cubed	675 g
2 cups	canned tomatoes with liquid	500 mL
1/2 cup	dry red wine	125 mL
14 oz	can artichoke hearts, drained and halved	398 mL
1 tbsp	chopped fresh oregano	15 mL
2 tbsp	chopped fresh parsley	30 mL
	salt and freshly ground pepper	

1 Heat oil in a large skillet. Add onion, garlic and pepper and cook over low heat about 5 minutes. Using a slotted spoon, transfer onion and garlic to a bowl.

2 Add pork to skillet and cook for 3 minutes over medium heat. Drain off excess fat.

3 Return onion mixture to pan. Add tomatoes and wine. Bring to a boil, then simmer, covered, about 20 minutes or until pork is tender. Stir in artichoke hearts, oregano and parsley. Season to taste. Heat through and serve immediately.

Serves 6

Lamb Stew *with* Lemon Sauce

1	lamb shoulder, boned	1
2	onions, chopped	2
1	red bell pepper, chopped	1
2	celery stalks, sliced	2
2 1/2 cups	chicken stock	625 mL
3 tbsp	butter	45 mL
2 tbsp	all-purpose flour	30 mL
2	egg yolks	2
1/4 cup	fresh lemon juice	60 mL
	salt and freshly ground pepper	
	fresh dill for garnish	

◆ ◆ ◆

1 Cut the lamb into 3/4 inch (2 cm) cubes. Trim and discard fat. Place cubed lamb in a large saucepan with onions, red pepper and celery. Add the stock. Bring to a boil. Skim until the surface is clear. Cover and simmer 1-1 1/2 hours or until lamb is tender.

2 Using a slotted spoon, transfer meat and vegetables to a deep serving dish and keep hot.

3 Strain the cooking liquid and measure out 1 1/2 cups (375 mL).

4 Melt butter in a medium saucepan. Add flour and stir over medium heat for 2 minutes. Gradually add measured stock, and stir until mixture boils and thickens slightly. Lower heat to a simmer.

5 In a bowl, whisk egg yolks together with lemon juice. Pour in about 1/4 cup (60 mL) of the hot stock mixture and whisk until smooth. Tip the egg yolk mixture into the saucepan with the rest of the stock. Stir constantly over low heat until mixture thickens further, but do not allow mixture to boil. Season to taste.

6 Pour sauce over the reserved meat and vegetables and mix lightly before serving, garnished with fresh dill.

Serves 6

Veal Rolls *in* Tomato Sauce

4	thin slices prosciutto	4
4	veal cutlets, tenderized (see Tip, page 32)	4
4 tbsp	grated Parmesan cheese	60 mL
4 tbsp	butter	60 mL
2 tbsp	olive oil	30 mL
1 cup	dry Marsala wine	250 mL
1 cup	canned tomatoes, puréed	250 mL
1 tbsp	chopped fresh parsley	15 mL
1	garlic clove, finely chopped	1

◆ ◆ ◆

1 Lay a slice of prosciutto on each veal cutlet, sprinkle with 1 tbsp (15 mL) Parmesan and roll up. Secure rolls with toothpicks.

2 Heat butter and oil in a large skillet. Add veal rolls and cook over medium-high heat until golden on all sides.

3 Stir in Marsala and cook until liquid is reduced by half. Transfer veal rolls to a plate and keep hot.

4 Add puréed tomatoes, parsley and garlic to liquid remaining in pan. Cook over medium heat for 5 minutes until sauce has thickened slightly.

5 Pour sauce onto a serving dish. Slice veal rolls crosswise and arrange on top of sauce. Garnish with parsley and serve immediately.

Serves 4

Lamb and Lemon Kebabs with Yogurt Sauce

4 tbsp	olive oil	60 mL
2	garlic cloves, finely chopped	2
2 tsp	ground cumin	10 mL
1 tsp	paprika	5 mL
5 tbsp	fresh lemon juice	75 mL
1 tsp	finely grated lemon zest	5 mL
1/4 cup	canned coconut milk	60 mL
1 1/2 lbs	lean lamb, cut in 3/4 inch (2 cm) cubes	675 g
1 tbsp	chopped fresh parsley	15 mL
1 cup	plain low-fat yogurt	250 mL
1 tbsp	chopped fresh mint	15 mL

♦ ♦ ♦

1 Combine oil, garlic, cumin, paprika, lemon juice, lemon zest and coconut milk in a large non-metallic bowl. Add lamb cubes. Mix well, cover, and refrigerate at least 6 hours and up to 24 hours.

2 Preheat broiler. Thread lamb onto presoaked wooden skewers. Broil for 3 minutes on each side or until cooked to taste. Sprinkle with parsley.

3 Combine yogurt and mint and serve with the lamb kebabs.

Serves 6

Pork *and* Herb Patties *with* Eggplant Sauce

¹/₂ lb	eggplant, peeled and diced	225 g
1 lb	lean ground pork	450 g
2	green onions, finely chopped	2
2	garlic cloves, finely chopped	2
2 tbsp	chopped fresh coriander	30 mL
³/₄ cup	fresh breadcrumbs	185 mL
1	egg, beaten	1
2 tbsp	olive oil	30 mL
2 tsp	ground cumin	10 mL
¹/₄ tsp	salt	1 mL
¹/₄ tsp	freshly ground pepper	1 mL
¹/₄ cup	sour cream	60 mL
	red bell pepper strips for garnish	

◆ ◆ ◆

1 Steam the eggplant until tender. Set aside.

2 Combine ground pork, green onions, garlic, coriander, breadcrumbs, and egg in a bowl. Mix well. Shape into 8 patties about ³/₄ inch (2 cm) thick.

3 Heat oil in a nonstick skillet over medium heat. Fry pork patties, in batches if necessary, 3-4 minutes on each side or until cooked through. Drain on paper towels and transfer to a warm plate. Keep hot.

4 Purée the eggplant with the cumin, salt and pepper in a blender or processor. Transfer the purée to a small saucepan. Stir in the sour cream and heat gently until warmed through. Do not allow mixture to boil. Serve the sauce over the patties and garnish with thin strips of red bell pepper.

Serves 4

Chicken with Olives and Tomatoes

4	chicken breast halves	4
2 tbsp	olive oil	30 mL
1 tbsp	butter, melted	15 mL
4	tomatoes, peeled, seeded and quartered	4
1/2 cup	stuffed green olives	125 mL
1/2 cup	black olives	125 mL
	freshly ground pepper	

♦ ♦ ♦

1 Preheat oven to 425°F (220°C). Pat chicken with paper towels and season well with pepper. Place in a baking dish and drizzle with olive oil. Bake, uncovered, 15-20 minutes or until cooked through.

2 Remove chicken and place on a heated serving dish. Spoon melted butter over chicken and keep warm.

3 Drain excess fat from baking dish and add tomatoes and olives. Return pan to the oven and bake for 5 minutes or until tomatoes are hot.

4 Arrange tomatoes and olives around the chicken and drizzle any juices remaining in the pan over them. Serve hot.

Serves 4

TIP: *This is a really fast and good main course when you want something a little exotic, but are pressed for time. Serve with rice or steamed parsley potatoes and a green salad.*

Chicken Marsala

4	boneless, skinless chicken breasts	4
1/2 cup	all-purpose flour	125 mL
5 tbsp	butter	75 mL
5 tbsp	Marsala wine	75 mL
3 tbsp	chopped chives	45 mL
	salt and freshly ground pepper	

♦ ♦ ♦

1 Cut each chicken breast in half to make 2 thin fillets. Coat chicken in flour, shaking off excess.

2 Melt 3 tbsp (45 mL) of butter in a heavy-based skillet until foaming. Add chicken to pan and cook over medium-high heat 1 minute on each side, or until golden-brown. Using tongs, transfer chicken to a dish, season with salt and pepper, and keep warm.

3 Pour out all but about 1 tbsp (15 mL) butter from the skillet. Add Marsala and boil for 1 minute, scraping up any browned bits on bottom of pan. Add remaining butter and any juices from reserved chicken.

4 Stir sauce over medium heat until it thickens. Return chicken to the pan and simmer until cooked through, basting frequently with sauce. Serve chicken pieces topped with sauce.

Serves 4

Chicken with Olives and Tomatoes

Chicken *with Bouillabaisse Sauce*

2 tbsp	olive oil	30 mL
2	onions, chopped	2
8	small chicken pieces such as drumsticks or thighs	8
8	tomatoes, peeled, seeded and chopped	8
3	garlic cloves, finely chopped	3
1	small bouquet garni	1
1	strip orange zest	1
1/4 tsp	fennel seeds	1 mL
1 tbsp	butter	15 mL
6	fresh basil leaves, chopped	6
1/2 tsp	saffron threads (optional)	2 mL
	salt and freshly ground pepper	

1 Heat olive oil in a large skillet over medium heat. Add onions and cook until soft and golden. Remove onions and set aside.

2 Add chicken pieces to pan. Cook until golden-brown on all sides. Season to taste with salt and pepper.

3 Add tomatoes, 2 chopped garlic cloves, bouquet garni, orange zest, and fennel. Stir to combine and season to taste. Cook, covered, 15-20 minutes or until chicken is tender.

4 Meanwhile, mash butter together with remaining garlic, basil and saffron, if desired. With a slotted spoon, transfer chicken pieces to a serving dish and set aside to keep warm. Whisk the butter mixture into the tomato mixture and gently heat through. To serve, pour sauce over chicken.

Serves 4

TIP: *A bouquet garni is an array of fresh or dried herbs tied together. The classic combination is thyme, parsley and bay leaves.*

Chicken and Vegetables with Basil

4 tbsp	olive oil	60 mL
4	boneless, skinless chicken breasts, cut in strips	4
1	rutabaga, cut in strips	1
2	onions, chopped	2
1	red bell pepper, cut in strips	1
1 cup	dry white wine	250 mL
2 cups	chopped canned tomatoes	500 mL
3 tbsp	chopped fresh basil	45 mL
	salt and freshly ground pepper	

◆ ◆ ◆

1 Heat oil in a large skillet. Add chicken strips and cook over medium heat for 2 minutes, stirring constantly. Using a slotted spoon, transfer chicken to a bowl and set aside.

2 Add rutabaga, onions and red pepper to the oil remaining in the pan. Cook 2-3 minutes, stirring occasionally.

3 Stir in wine and tomatoes. Bring to a boil, then lower heat and simmer for 10 minutes uncovered. Season to taste.

4 Stir in chicken and chopped basil. Heat through for 1 minute. Serve garnished with fresh basil leaves, if desired.

Serves 4

Quail with Caper Dill Sauce

1 tbsp	butter	15 mL
1	onion, sliced	1
1	garlic clove, finely chopped	1
1	red bell pepper, cut in thin strips	1
1 tbsp	liquid honey	15 mL
2 tbsp	red wine vinegar	30 mL
4	quails, cut in half lengthwise	4
1 cup	dry white wine	250 mL
2 tsp	Dijon mustard	10 mL
1 tbsp	chopped fresh dill	15 mL
1/2 tsp	crushed black peppercorns	2 mL
1 tbsp	capers	15 mL
	fresh thyme	

1 In a large skillet, melt butter over medium heat. Add onion, garlic, and pepper strips. Cook for 2 minutes.

2 Add honey, wine vinegar, and quails. Cook quails for 3 minutes on each side.

3 Add wine, mustard, dill, pepper and capers. Cook until sauce thickens slightly and quails are cooked through.

4 Arrange 2 quail halves on each plate. Spoon sauce over the top. Garnish with fresh thyme and serve.

Serves 4

♦ ♦ ♦

Chicken with Peppers and Yogurt

6 tbsp	olive oil	90 mL
6	chicken pieces	6
1	onion, cut in wedges	1
3	garlic cloves, finely chopped	3
1	red bell pepper, cut in strips	1
1	yellow or green bell pepper, cut in strips	1
4	tomatoes, peeled and chopped	4
1 tbsp	paprika	15 mL
1/2 cup	dry white wine	125 mL
3/4 cup	plain yogurt	185 mL
	salt and freshly ground pepper	
	chopped fresh parsley	

♦ ♦ ♦

1 Heat 3 tbsp (45 mL) oil in a large saucepan over medium heat. Add chicken pieces and cook until golden-brown on all sides. Remove chicken and set aside. Keep warm.

2 Add onion, garlic, and red and yellow pepper strips to pan. Cook for 5 minutes, stirring occasionally, until soft.

3 Add tomatoes, paprika, and wine. Stir well. Return chicken to pan. Spoon sauce over and simmer, covered, for about 30 minutes or until chicken is tender. Season to taste.

4 To serve, arrange chicken on a warmed serving dish, top with vegetable mixture, drizzle with yogurt and sprinkle with chopped parsley.

Serves 4-6

RICE, PASTA
AND POLENTA

Pasta and rice form the basis of some of the most delicious dishes to emerge from the Mediterranean region. Together with polenta, they provide the perfect vehicle for a range of superb sauces.

Please note that the portion sizes in this chapter are for starter size or side-dish servings, especially when it comes to the pasta recipes. If you want to use these recipes for a main course, they will serve 2-3 people.

POLENTA WITH MUSHROOM SAUCE, WILD RICE AND MUSHROOMS (PAGE 48)

Wild Rice and Mushrooms

2 tbsp	butter	30 mL
4	green onions, chopped	4
1	leek, white part only, thinly sliced	1
4 oz	mushrooms, sliced	120 g
8 oz	wild rice, washed and drained	240 g
2 1/2 cups	chicken stock	625 mL
	salt	

❖ ◆ ❖

1 Melt butter in a large skillet. Add green onions, leek and mushrooms. Cook over medium heat for 3 minutes, stirring frequently. Remove vegetables with a slotted spoon and set aside.

2 Add wild rice to butter remaining in pan. Stir until well coated. Add stock, bring to a boil, then simmer for 30-40 minutes until rice is tender and liquid has been absorbed.

3 Stir reserved vegetables into rice. Taste and add salt if necessary. Heat through and serve immediately.

Serves 4

Polenta with Mushroom Sauce

1 1/4 cups	milk	310 mL
1 1/4 cups	water	310 mL
1 tsp	crushed black peppercorns	5 mL
1	garlic clove, finely chopped	1
3/4 cup	polenta (yellow cornmeal)	185 mL
1/2 cup	grated Parmesan cheese	125 mL
	pinch salt	

MUSHROOM SAUCE

2 tsp	olive oil	10 mL
1	onion, chopped	1
1	garlic clove, finely chopped	1
1/4 lb	mushrooms, sliced	110 g
1/4 tsp	chili powder	1 mL
1 cup	chopped canned tomatoes	250 mL
	fresh thyme for garnish	

❖ ◆ ❖

1 Combine milk, water, pepper, salt and garlic in a small saucepan. Bring to a boil. Simmer, stirring, for 10-15 minutes. Strain liquid into a medium saucepan.

2 Stir in polenta. Stir over medium heat until boiling, then reduce heat and simmer, stirring constantly, for 10-15 minutes or until mixture starts to thicken and come away from sides of pan.

3 Spoon polenta into 8-inch (20 cm) round baking dish. Spread evenly. Set aside to cool.

4 Preheat oven to 350°F (180°C). Sprinkle Parmesan over polenta. Bake 15 minutes. Cut into serving wedges and place on a serving plate. Keep hot.

5 To make the mushroom sauce, heat oil in a skillet over medium-high heat. Add onion, garlic, mushrooms and chili powder. Cook for 3 minutes. Stir in tomatoes and cook for 3 minutes more. Pour sauce into a serving bowl and serve with polenta, garnished with a sprig of thyme.

Serves 4

Baked Cheese Polenta with Spicy Meat Sauce

3 cups	each milk and water	750 mL
2 tsp	salt	10 mL
2 cups	polenta (yellow cornmeal)	500 mL
2 cups	grated Parmesan cheese	500 mL

MEAT SAUCE

1 tbsp	butter	15 mL
1	onion, chopped	1
2	garlic cloves, chopped	2
1 lb	ground beef	450 g
1 cup	dry white wine	250 mL
2 tbsp	tomato paste	30 mL
2 cups	chopped canned tomatoes	500 mL
1 tsp	dried basil	5 mL
1	bay leaf	1
1 cup	puréed tomatoes	250 mL
2 tbsp	Worcestershire sauce	30 mL

◆ ◆ ◆

1 To make sauce, melt butter in a large saucepan over medium heat. Add onion and garlic; cook 3 minutes. Stir in ground beef and brown on all sides.

2 Add wine. Stir over high heat 10 minutes. Stir in remaining sauce ingredients, lower heat, and simmer for 25 minutes, stirring occasionally.

3 Meanwhile, make the polenta. Combine milk and water in a large saucepan. Add salt and bring to a boil, then lower heat to a simmer. Very slowly pour in polenta in a thin stream, stirring constantly and rapidly. Cook mixture, stirring constantly, for 15 minutes.

4 Preheat oven to 350°F (180°C). Line a greased 8-inch (20 cm) springform pan with foil. Grease the foil.

5 Remove saucepan from heat, stir Parmesan into the polenta, and pour into prepared pan. Bake for 20 minutes. Serve polenta in wedges topped with meat sauce. Garnish with fresh basil if desired.

Serves 6-8

Mushroom Risotto *with* Sausage Bolognese

4 tbsp	butter or olive oil	60 mL
1	onion, finely chopped	1
1/2 lb	mushrooms, sliced	225 g
2	garlic cloves, finely chopped	2
1 cup	short-grain rice	250 mL
2 1/2 cups	chicken stock	625 mL
	salt	

SAUCE BOLOGNESE

1 tbsp	olive oil	15 mL
1	onion, finely chopped	1
4	Italian sausages, casings removed	4
3/4 cup	puréed tomatoes	185 mL
2 cups	chopped canned tomatoes	500 mL
1 tsp	Italian herbs	5 mL
	salt and freshly ground pepper	

1 Melt butter in a large deep skillet over medium heat. Add onion and mushrooms. Cook 5 minutes, stirring occasionally. Add garlic and rice. Stir well and cook 2 minutes more.

2 Stir in stock and salt to taste. Bring to a boil, then lower heat and simmer, uncovered, for 15 minutes, stirring occasionally until most of the liquid has been absorbed. If still very moist, raise heat to high and cook 4-5 minutes, stirring constantly.

3 Meanwhile, to make the sauce, heat oil in a saucepan over medium heat. Add onion and crumbled sausage meat. Cook, stirring, for 7 minutes. Drain off excess oil. Stir in puréed tomatoes, chopped tomatoes and herbs with salt and pepper to taste. Simmer another 7 minutes.

4 Transfer risotto to a serving dish, top with bolognese sauce and serve at once.

◆ ◆ ◆

Serves 4

Potato *and* Cheese Gnocchi

2 lbs	potatoes, peeled and cubed	1 kg
1 cup	all-purpose flour	250 mL
2 cups	grated Parmesan cheese	500 mL
3 cups	grated Emmenthal cheese	750 mL
2 tbsp	butter, melted	30 mL
	salt	

1 Bring a large saucepan of lightly salted water to a boil. Add potatoes and cook until very tender. Drain thoroughly, then mash until fluffy. Beat in flour with an electric mixer, mixing well.

2 Roll teaspoonfuls of the mixture into balls. Press each ball lightly with the tines of a fork to flatten slightly.

3 Preheat oven to 350°F (180°C). Bring a large saucepan of water to a boil. Drop in a quarter of the gnocchi and cook until they rise to the surface. As each gnocchi bobs to the surface, remove it with a slotted spoon.

4 Repeat with remaining batches of gnocchi. Layer them in a baking dish between layers of Parmesan and Emmenthal, ending with a layer of cheese. Pour in melted butter. Bake for 15 minutes or until cheese is melted and bubbling. Serve at once.

Serves 6

Spirelli with Tomato and Artichoke Sauce

1 tbsp	olive oil	15 mL
1	onion, chopped	1
2	garlic cloves, finely chopped	2
4	large ripe tomatoes, peeled and chopped	4
2 tbsp	chopped fresh basil	30 mL
2 tbsp	chopped fresh parsley	30 mL
14 oz	can artichoke hearts, drained and halved	398 mL
12 oz	spirelli pasta	360 g
	basil sprigs and grated Parmesan cheese	

◆ ◆ ◆

1 Heat oil in a saucepan, add onion and garlic and sauté over low heat until tender. Stir in tomatoes, basil and parsley. Bring to a boil, lower heat, and simmer about 30 minutes until sauce has reduced and thickened. Stir in artichoke halves.

2 Cook spirelli in boiling salted water according to package directions. Drain well. Top with sauce. Garnish with basil and serve with Parmesan cheese.

Serves 4

Tagliatelle and Potatoes with Garlic and Olive Oil

2	large baking potatoes	2
12 oz	tagliatelle pasta	360 g
1 cup	olive oil	250 mL
10	garlic cloves, finely chopped	10
1	hot red chili pepper, seeded and chopped	1
4 tbsp	chopped fresh parsley	60 mL
	salt and freshly ground pepper	

◆ ◆ ◆

1 Preheat oven to 400°F (200°C). Bake potatoes for 40-50 minutes or until tender. When cool, peel and cut in 1/4 inch (5 mm) slices.

2 Cook tagliatelle in boiling salted water until *al dente*. Drain.

3 Heat oil in a large saucepan. Add garlic, chili and potatoes and cook over medium heat for 5 minutes or until potatoes are golden.

4 Add tagliatelle to pan and stir. Season to taste and serve hot, sprinkled with parsley.

Serves 4

NOTE: *This is the perfect example of a terrific dish made with ordinary (and possibly leftover, when it comes to the potatoes) ingredients. Give it a try!*

Spirelli with Tomato and Artichoke Sauce

Fettucine *with* Red Pepper *and* Goats' Cheese

12 oz	fettucine pasta	360 g
2 tbsp	olive oil	30 mL
2	garlic cloves, finely chopped	2
2	red bell peppers, cut in thin strips	2
8	green onions, cut in thin strips	8
1/2 tsp	coarsely ground black pepper	2 mL
4 oz	goats' cheese, crumbled	120 g

◆ ◆ ◆

1 Bring a large saucepan of water to a boil. Add the fettucine and cook until *al dente*.

2 Meanwhile, heat oil in a large deep skillet over medium heat. Add garlic and red peppers and cook for 2 minutes; do not allow garlic to burn. Add green onions and pepper and cook 1 minute more.

3 Drain pasta and add to the red pepper mixture. Toss well. Carefully stir in cheese. Divide pasta between 4 heated plates and serve at once.

Serves 4

Spaghetti with Pesto

2 oz	fresh basil leaves	60 g
3 tbsp	pine nuts	45 mL
4	garlic cloves, finely chopped	4
1/2 tsp	sugar	2 mL
1/2 tsp	salt	2 mL
5 tbsp	olive oil	75 mL
12 oz	spaghetti	360 g

◆ ◆ ◆

1 Combine basil, pine nuts, garlic, sugar, and salt in a blender or food processor. Process briefly to mix. With motor running, gradually add olive oil through the feeder tube. The mixture will form a thick sauce. Scrape into a bowl and set aside.

2 Cook spaghetti in lightly salted boiling water until *al dente*. Drain and tip into a heated bowl. Add pesto and toss until evenly coated. Serve at once, garnished with fresh basil leaves.

Serves 6

VEGETABLES
AND SALADS

Visit any Mediterranean market and marvel at the colorful array of vegetables. Deep purple eggplants, red, green and yellow peppers, tomatoes, bunches of glossy green spinach — the selection might lack the cool crispness of some northern varieties, but it is an open invitation to create a meal that looks as good as it tastes.

This chapter contains a selection of interesting cooked vegetable dishes with a Mediterranean twist. We have also included a selection of great salads — some well-known, and others that are sure to become favorites!

Potatoes with Red Peppers, Peas with Prosciutto (page 58)

Potatoes with Red Peppers

3	large potatoes, cut in 1/4 inch (5 mm) slices	3
2	onions, chopped	2
2	red bell peppers, cut in thin strips	2
2	slices bacon, cut in thin strips	2
1 tbsp	chopped fresh sage	15 mL
1/2 tsp	crushed black peppercorns	2 mL
1/4 cup	olive oil	60 mL
	salt	
	fresh sage for garnish	

♦ ◆ ♦

1 Preheat oven to 350°F (180°C). Mix potatoes, onions, red peppers and bacon in a large baking dish.

2 Combine sage, peppercorns, salt to taste and olive oil in a bowl. Pour mixture over potatoes. Bake for 40 minutes, turning vegetables occasionally. Garnish with fresh sage and serve.

Serves 6

Peas with Prosciutto

3 tbsp	olive oil	45 mL
2 tbsp	butter	30 mL
1	onion, chopped	1
6	slices prosciutto, chopped	6
1 lb	shelled peas	450 g
1 cup	water	250 mL
1 tbsp	chopped fresh mint	15 mL
	salt and freshly ground pepper	
	mint sprig for garnish	

♦ ◆ ♦

1 Heat oil and butter together in a large skillet. Add onion and prosciutto and cook for 3 minutes over medium heat.

2 Add peas and water. Bring to a boil, then lower heat. Simmer peas for about 20 minutes or until tender.

3 Strain peas and transfer to a serving dish. Toss with chopped mint, and salt and pepper to taste. Serve garnished with a mint sprig.

Serves 4

TIP: You can easily use frozen peas in this recipe, but if you do, cut the amount of water to 1/4 cup (60 mL).

Tian Rouge

3	red bell peppers, halved	3
4 tbsp	chopped fresh Italian parsley	60 mL
3 tbsp	chopped fresh basil	45 mL
2 tbsp	chopped fresh thyme	30 mL
4	green onions, finely chopped	4
1 cup	dry breadcrumbs	250 mL
6	large ripe tomatoes, peeled and sliced ³/4 inch (2 cm) thick	6
1 tbsp	capers	15 mL
	olive oil	
	breadcrumbs	
	salt and freshly ground pepper	

♦ ♦ ♦

1 Brush halved peppers with oil, place under a preheated broiler, and broil until skin is charred. Place peppers in a paper bag until cool, then rub off charred skin and cut out seeds and membranes. Slice peppers into ³/4 inch (2 cm) strips.

2 Combine parsley, herbs, onions and breadcrumbs in a bowl. Place one-third of the tomato slices in an oiled, ovenproof baking dish. Sprinkle with one-third of crumb mixture. Season to taste with salt and pepper and sprinkle with a little olive oil. Cover with half the pepper strips.

3 Repeat layers, then top with remaining tomato slices and herb mixture. Sprinkle top with capers and extra breadcrumbs. Drizzle with oil.

4 Preheat oven to 350°F (180°C). Bake tian for 20-25 minutes or until bubbly and browned. Let cool, and serve chilled or at room temperature.

Serves 6

TIP: *When you don't have fresh herbs, substitute 1 tsp (5 mL) dried herbs for each tbsp (15 mL) of the fresh herbs called for in the recipe.*

Layered Eggplant and Artichokes

2	eggplants, cut into thin slices	2
2 tbsp	olive oil	30 mL
2	onions, sliced	2
2	garlic cloves, finely chopped	2
1 1/2 cups	chopped canned tomatoes	375 mL
2 tsp	Italian herbs	10 mL
14 oz	can artichoke hearts, drained and coarsely chopped	398 mL
2	tomatoes, sliced	2
1/2 cup	cottage cheese	125 mL
1/2 cup	ricotta cheese	125 mL
1/2 cup	grated aged cheddar cheese	125 mL
1	egg white	1
1/4 cup	milk	60 mL

1 Preheat oven to 350°F (180°C). Place 1/2 cup (125 mL) water in a large skillet over medium heat. Add eggplant slices and cook for 3 minutes. Remove with a slotted spoon and drain on paper towels.

2 Heat oil in a skillet and add onions and garlic. Cook 2 minutes over medium heat. Add tomatoes and herbs. Simmer 5-7 minutes until thickened. Stir in artichoke hearts.

3 Arrange half the tomato slices over the bottom of an oiled baking dish. Top with half the eggplant slices, then half of tomato sauce mixture. Repeat layers.

4 In a food processor or blender, combine cheeses, egg white and milk until smooth. Spread over vegetables. Bake 30 minutes. Serve hot.

Serves 4

Baked Fennel *with Caper Sauce*

2	medium fennel bulbs, sliced lengthwise 3/4 inch (2 cm) thick	2
2 tbsp	olive oil	30 mL
2 tbsp	butter	30 mL
2	garlic cloves, finely chopped	2
1	onion, chopped	1
2 cups	chopped canned tomatoes	500 mL
3 tbsp	tomato paste	45 mL
1 tbsp	drained capers	15 mL
1/4 cup	dry white wine	60 mL
1 tbsp	chopped fresh basil	15 mL

♦ ♦ ♦

1 Preheat oven to 350°F (180°C). Arrange fennel in a greased baking dish, brush with olive oil, and bake for 25 minutes.

2 Melt butter in a skillet. Add garlic and onion. Cook over low heat for 5 minutes. Stir in tomatoes, tomato paste, capers, wine and basil. Bring to a boil. Lower heat and simmer for 15 minutes, stirring occasionally. Serve sauce over fennel.

Serves 4

Eggplant Provençale

2	large eggplants, halved lengthwise	2
2 tbsp	olive oil	30 mL
1	onion, chopped	1
2	garlic cloves, finely chopped	2
2	slices bacon, chopped (optional)	2
1/2 cup	chopped canned tomatoes	125 mL
1 tsp	chopped fresh thyme	5 mL
1	egg	1
1/2 cup	dry breadcrumbs	125 mL
2 cups	cooked rice	500 mL
1 cup	grated Parmesan cheese	250 mL
	salt	

♦ ♦ ♦

1 Scoop flesh from eggplant halves without piercing skins, leaving a 3/4 inch (2 cm) thick shell. Sprinkle with salt and invert on paper towels. Set aside for 15 minutes.

2 Combine remaining ingredients. Season to taste.

3 Preheat oven to 350°F (180°C). Rinse eggplant shells and pat dry with paper towels. Spoon filling into eggplant shells. Arrange in a baking pan and bake for 30 minutes. Serve hot.

Serves 4

Potato and Zucchini Bake

1 lb	potatoes, cut into large chunks	450 g
2 tbsp	olive oil	30 mL
4	zucchini, sliced	4
1	onion, chopped	1
2	garlic cloves, finely chopped	2
4	tomatoes, chopped	4
1 tbsp	chopped fresh basil	15 mL
2 tsp	chopped fresh oregano	10 mL
1 cup	fresh wholewheat breadcrumbs	250 mL
1 cup	grated Parmesan cheese	250 mL

◆ ◆ ◆

1 Preheat oven to 350°F (180°C). Cook potatoes in boiling salted water until tender. Drain and spoon into 4 individual baking dishes (or 1 larger dish).

2 Heat 1 tbsp (15 mL) oil in a skillet over medium heat. Add zucchini and stir-fry until tender. Add to potatoes.

3 Heat remaining oil in skillet. Add onion and garlic and cook until tender. Add tomatoes, basil and oregano. Cook to a sauce-like consistency. Pour over potato and zucchini mixture. Combine breadcrumbs and cheese. Divide over baking dishes. Bake for 30 minutes until the topping is golden-brown.

Serves 4

TIP: This is one of those recipes to keep up your sleeve when you want a make-ahead potato dish. Refrigerate and then add a few minutes to the baking time.

SALADE NIÇOISE

Salade Niçoise

2 cups	green beans, trimmed	500 mL
6 oz	can solid tuna in oil, drained	180 g
1 cup	cherry tomatoes, quartered	250 mL
4	hard-boiled eggs, sliced	4
12	pitted black olives	12
8	canned anchovy fillets, drained	8
1 tbsp	chopped chives	15 mL
1 tbsp	drained capers	15 mL
2 tbsp	olive oil	30 mL
2 tbsp	vinaigrette	30 mL
1	garlic clove, finely chopped	1

1 Cook beans for 1 minute in boiling salted water. Drain, refresh under cold water, drain again and set aside.

2 Break up tuna into chunks. Arrange beans, tuna, tomatoes, egg slices, olives and anchovies in salad bowls. Sprinkle with chives and capers. Dress with a mixture of olive oil, vinaigrette and chopped garlic.

Serves 4

TIP: *A more substantial variation of this salad involves adding about 2 cups (500 mL) cubed cooked potatoes.*

◆ ◆ ◆

Vinaigrette

2 tbsp	wine vinegar	30 mL
1 tsp	Dijon mustard	5 mL
1/4 tsp	salt	1 mL
6 tbsp	olive oil	90 mL
	freshly ground pepper	

1 Combine all ingredients in a small screw-top jar, and shake until well mixed.

◆ ◆ ◆

Radicchio and Broccoli Salad

1	red bell pepper, cut in thin strips	1
1/2 lb	broccoli florets	225 g
1	radicchio lettuce, shredded	1
4 tbsp	pine nuts, toasted	60 mL
4 tbsp	olive oil	60 mL
2 tbsp	red wine vinegar	30 mL
1 tbsp	fresh lemon juice	15 mL
1/4 tsp	crushed black peppercorns	1 mL

1 Place pepper strips in a bowl of ice water and refrigerate 15 minutes until they curl.

2 Meanwhile, bring a large pot of salted water to a boil, add broccoli and cook for 1 minute. Drain, refresh under cold water and drain again. Arrange radicchio on a salad plate. Top with broccoli and pine nuts.

3 Whisk together olive oil, vinegar, lemon juice and pepper. Pour over broccoli and toss lightly. Top with red pepper curls.

Serves 4

◆ ◆ ◆

Marinated Mushroom *and* Red Pepper Salad

2	red bell peppers, halved	2
2 tbsp	lemon juice	30 mL
1 tbsp	red wine vinegar	15 mL
2	garlic cloves, finely chopped	2
1 tbsp	chopped fresh basil	15 mL
1 tbsp	chopped fresh parsley	15 mL
4 tbsp	olive oil	60 mL
1/2 lb	mushrooms, sliced	225 g
	fresh basil for garnish	

♦ ♦ ♦

1 Place peppers under a preheated broiler, and broil until skin is charred. Place peppers in a paper bag until cool, then rub off charred skin and remove seeds and membranes. Slice peppers into strips and set aside.

2 Combine lemon juice, red wine vinegar, garlic, basil, parsley and oil in a large bowl. Whisk well.

3 Stir in reserved pepper strips and mushrooms. Cover and chill 3 hours. Serve garnished with fresh basil.

Serves 4

Greek Country Salad

2	cucumbers, sliced	2
1/2 lb	cherry tomatoes	225 g
1	onion, thinly sliced into rings	1
1	green bell pepper, cut into thin strips	1
3/4 cup	black olives	185 mL
6 oz	feta cheese, diced	180 g
5 tbsp	olive oil	75 mL
1/2 tsp	crushed black peppercorns	2 mL
2 tbsp	fresh lemon juice	30 mL

1 In a large serving bowl, toss together cucumber slices, tomatoes, onion rings, and green pepper strips. Scatter with olives and feta. (Alternatively, you can arrange the ingredients neatly on individual salad plates.)

2 Whisk together oil, pepper and lemon juice. Pour over salad and toss lightly to coat.

Serves 6

Radicchio Salad with *Sun-Dried Tomatoes and Artichokes*

1	radicchio lettuce	1
2 cups	loosely packed fresh parsley sprigs	500 mL
6 oz	feta cheese, diced	180 g
14 oz	can artichoke hearts, drained and halved	398 mL
3 oz	sun-dried tomatoes in oil, drained and chopped	90 g
1 tbsp	fresh lemon juice	15 mL
3 tbsp	olive oil	45 mL

♦ ♦ ♦

1 Arrange lettuce leaves and parsley sprigs on individual plates. Top with feta, artichoke halves and sun-dried tomatoes.

2 Whisk together lemon juice and olive oil. Drizzle over salad and serve.

Serves 4-6

Tomato and Basil Salad

2	large tomatoes, sliced and halved	2
1 oz	fresh basil leaves	30 g
1	red onion, sliced into rings	1
DRESSING		
2	garlic cloves, finely chopped	2
2 tsp	olive oil	10 mL
1 tbsp	freshly squeezed lime juice	15 mL
1/2 tsp	crushed black peppercorns	2 mL

◆ ◆ ◆

1. Arrange tomato slices alternately with basil leaves around each salad plate.

2. Place onion rings in the center of each plate. Shake together the dressing ingredients and pour over salad.

Serves 4

TIP: *Don't be fooled by the simplicity of this salad. It is the best possible way to treat home-grown or market garden tomatoes in season.*

DESSERTS

Desserts are not a universal feature of Mediterranean meals. In Greece, for instance, it is customary to enjoy sweet treats such as baklava in the late afternoon with coffee; if anything sweet is served after lunch or dinner, it is likely to be fresh fruit.

But everywhere in the Mediterranean, the approach to meals is a leisurely one, with plenty of time for dessert if that is your preference. And these recipes are so fast and simple that you can take a leisurely approach to making dessert, too!

PLUM AND APRICOT CLAFOUTI (PAGE 72)

Plum and Apricot Clafouti

4 tbsp	self-raising flour	60 mL
6 tbsp	all-purpose flour	90 mL
1 tsp	sugar	5 mL
3/4 cup	ground almonds	185 mL
2	eggs	2
4 tbsp	butter, melted	60 mL
2/3 cup	milk	150 mL
2 tbsp	icing sugar	30 mL
6	plums, pitted and coarsely chopped	6
6	apricots, pitted and coarsely chopped	6
	icing sugar for dusting	

1 Preheat oven to 350°F (180°C). Sift flours together into a medium bowl. Stir in sugar and almonds. Make a well in the center.

2 In another bowl, mix together eggs, butter and milk. Pour into well in dry mixture. Gradually stir flour into liquid until batter is smooth.

3 Lightly grease a 9 inch (23 cm) quiche pan. Sprinkle with icing sugar, shaking off excess. Spread plum and apricot pieces evenly over base of dish.

4 Pour batter over fruit. Bake for 25-30 minutes. Dust with icing sugar.

Serves 6

♦ ♦ ♦

Pears with Ricotta and Walnuts

1 1/2 cups	ricotta cheese	375 mL
1/4 cup	whipping cream	60 mL
1/4 cup	nut-flavored liqueur (optional)	60 mL
4 tbsp	chopped fresh mint	60 mL
6	pears, peeled, halved and cored	6
12	walnut halves, coarsely chopped	12
	mint sprigs for garnish	

1 In a bowl, combine cheese, cream and liqueur, if desired. Add chopped mint and beat mixture until smooth.

2 Arrange pears on 6 dessert plates. Top each with some of the cheese mixture, sprinkle with walnuts, and garnish with mint sprigs.

Serves 6

TIP: The pears for this dessert should be perfectly ripe but still relatively firm. Avoid any that are bruised.

♦ ♦ ♦

Champagne Zabaglione *with* Oranges

2	large navel oranges, peeled, segmented, all membranes removed	2
3	large egg yolks	3
2 tbsp	sugar	30 mL
1/4 tsp	cinnamon	1 mL
1/2 cup	champagne or dry sparkling wine	125 mL

1 Drain orange segments well.

2 Place egg yolks, sugar and cinnamon in a bowl set over a saucepan of simmering water (or in the top of a double boiler) and whisk until mixture is pale yellow and slightly thickened.

3 Add half the champagne and continue to whisk until foamy. Add remaining champagne. Beat another 5 minutes.

4 Divide orange segments between 4 serving glasses. Spoon sauce over oranges and garnish with fresh mint, if desired.

Serves 4

Berries with Mascarpone

3 cups	blueberries or raspberries	750 mL
2 cups	strawberries, hulled and quartered	500 mL
2 tbsp	brandy	30 mL
1 tbsp	liquid honey	15 mL
2 tbsp	freshly squeezed lime juice	30 mL
4 tbsp	freshly squeezed orange juice	60 mL
1 1/2 cups	mascarpone cheese	375 mL
	broken caramel pieces for decoration (optional)	

◆ ◆ ◆

1 Place blueberries or raspberries in bottom of 4 serving dishes. Top with strawberries.

2 Mix together brandy, honey, lime juice and orange juice. Pour over berries.

3 Spoon mascarpone on top and decorate with shards of caramel, if desired.

Serves 4

TIP: To make caramel, boil 1/2 cup (125 mL) white sugar gently in a small saucepan until bubbly, clear and light brown in color. Pour onto a lightly oiled baking sheet. When cold and brittle, break it up with a rolling pin or meat pounder. Dislodge pieces with a metal spatula. Store in an airtight jar.

French Apple Tarts

1/2 lb	readymade puff pastry, thawed	225 g
1	egg yolk, beaten	1
2	baking apples, peeled, cored and thinly sliced	2
1 tbsp	liquid honey	15 mL
1 tbsp	sugar	15 mL
	whipped cream	

◆ ◆ ◆

1 Preheat oven to 375°F (190°C). Cut pastry into 4 squares. Cut a 1/4 inch (5 mm) strip from each side of each square. Brush squares with egg yolk. Place pastry strips around edge of each square to make a raised edge, as shown.

2 Brush each pastry case with egg yolk. Place on dampened baking sheet and bake 10 minutes.

3 Arrange apple slices in center of each pastry case. Brush with honey and sprinkle with sugar.

4 Bake for 15 minutes. Serve immediately with whipped cream.

Serves 4

RICOTTA CUSTARD

Ricotta Custard

4	ladyfinger cookies	4
2 tbsp	Amaretto or other almond-flavored liqueur	30 mL
4	eggs	4
1/2 cup	sugar	125 mL
1 cup	ricotta cheese	250 mL
2 tsp	vanilla extract	10 mL
1/4 cup	icing sugar	60 mL

◆ ◆ ◆

1 Place a ladyfinger in each dessert dish. Drizzle with liqueur and set aside.

2 In a bowl, beat eggs together with sugar until light and fluffy.

3 Combine ricotta, vanilla and icing sugar in a blender or food processor. Process until smooth. Scrape into bowl containing egg mixture. Beat until well combined.

4 Divide mixture between the 4 dessert dishes. Chill 30 minutes before serving.

Serves 4

Orange Cream Cheese Filled Figs

8	whole candied figs	8
5 oz	cream cheese, softened	150 g
2 tsp	grated orange zest	10 mL
2 tbsp	orange-flavored liqueur	30 mL
1/4 cup	icing sugar	60 mL
SYRUP		
1/2 cup	freshly squeezed orange juice	125 mL
1 tbsp	lemon juice	15 mL
2 tbsp	sugar	30 mL

◆ ◆ ◆

1 Slit the figs open lengthwise. To make the filling, beat cream cheese with orange zest, liqueur and icing sugar until creamy. Spoon equal amounts of mixture into the figs. Arrange 2 figs on each of 4 dessert plates. Cover and chill.

2 Meanwhile, to make the syrup, combine juices and sugar in a small, heavy-based saucepan over low heat. Bring slowly to a boil. Simmer for 5 minutes. Set aside to cool for 15 minutes. Serve with the chilled figs.

Serves 4

TIP: Serve the same cream-cheese filling in fresh peach halves.

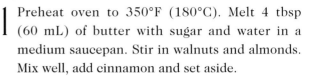

Baklava

¹/₄ lb	butter	110 g
6 tbsp	sugar	90 mL
5 oz	water	150 mL
1 cup	chopped walnuts	250 mL
1 cup	chopped blanched almonds	250 mL
¹/₄ tsp	ground cinnamon	1 mL
12	sheets filo pastry	12

SYRUP

1 cup	sugar	250 mL
²/₃ cup	water	165 mL
2 tbsp	lemon juice	30 mL

◆ ◆ ◆

1 Preheat oven to 350°F (180°C). Melt 4 tbsp (60 mL) of butter with sugar and water in a medium saucepan. Stir in walnuts and almonds. Mix well, add cinnamon and set aside.

2 Melt remaining butter. Use some of it to grease a 7 x 11 inch (18 x 28 cm) baking pan. Line pan with 4 sheets of filo, brushing each sheet with melted butter.

3 Spread half of nut mixture over filo in pan. Cover with 4 more filo sheets, brushing each with butter. Cover with remaining nut mixture, then 4 last filo sheets, brushing each with butter.

4 Using a sharp knife, cut surface layers of pastry in diamond shapes. Bake for 40 minutes.

5 Meanwhile, make syrup by mixing all ingredients in a saucepan. Bring to a boil and boil gently 5 minutes. Let cool slightly.

6 Pour syrup over baked baklava as soon as it is removed from oven. Set aside to cool. Allow to stand 2-3 hours before serving, but do not chill.

Serves 10

TIP: *A variation of this baklava omits the almonds and uses 2 cups (500 mL) walnuts. Add 4 tbsp (60 mL) liquid honey to the syrup and increase the quantity of lemon juice to 3 tbsp (45 mL).*

Fresh Figs with Orange and Grand Marnier

12	slightly underripe green or purple figs	12
1 cup	fresh orange juice	250 mL
¼ cup	Grand Marnier	60 mL

◆ ◆ ◆

1 Remove stems from the figs and cut them into quarters lengthwise. Place in a medium bowl and pour orange juice and Grand Marnier over top. Cover and refrigerate overnight.

2 Transfer to a glass serving dish or individual dessert dishes and serve.

Serves 6

TIP: This is one of those recipes where ultimate success depends on the quality of the ingredients. Don't give in to the temptation to use reconstituted orange juice instead of squeezing your own! You should need only 2 or 3 good juice oranges.

INDEX